Recycled
HEXIE Quilts

Mary W. Kerr

Schiffer Publishing Ltd

4880 Lower Valley Road • Atglen, PA 19310

Other Schiffer Books on related subjects:

World War I Quilts
ISBN: 978-0-7643-4754-2

Quilts in Everyday life, 1855–1955:
A Photographic History
ISBN: 978-0-7643-4612-5

Other Schiffer Books by the Author:

Dare to Dance
ISBN: 978-0-7643-4612-5

Published by Schiffer Publishing, Ltd.
4880 Lower Valley Road
Atglen, PA 19310
Phone: (610) 593-1777; Fax: (610) 593-2002
E-mail: Info@schifferbooks.com

For our complete selection of fine books on this and related subjects, please visit our website at www.schifferbooks.com. You may also write for a free catalog.

This book may be purchased from the publisher. Please try your bookstore first.

We are always looking for people to write books on new and related subjects. If you have an idea for a book, please contact us at proposals@schifferbooks.com.

Schiffer Publishing's titles are available at special discounts for bulk purchases for sales promotions or premiums. Special editions, including personalized covers, corporate imprints, and excerpts can be created in large quantities for special needs. For more information, contact the publisher.

Designed by RoS
Type set in Helvetica Neue LT Pro/Archer

ISBN: 978-0-7643-4820-4
Printed in The United States of America

dedication

To the quilt makers of yesteryear who left us such wonderful pieces to admire, appreciate, and enjoy.

To those who love and support us today as we work to celebrate our place in this quilting community.

To those who have gone before us, now smiling down and encouraging from above.

You are missed but never forgotten.

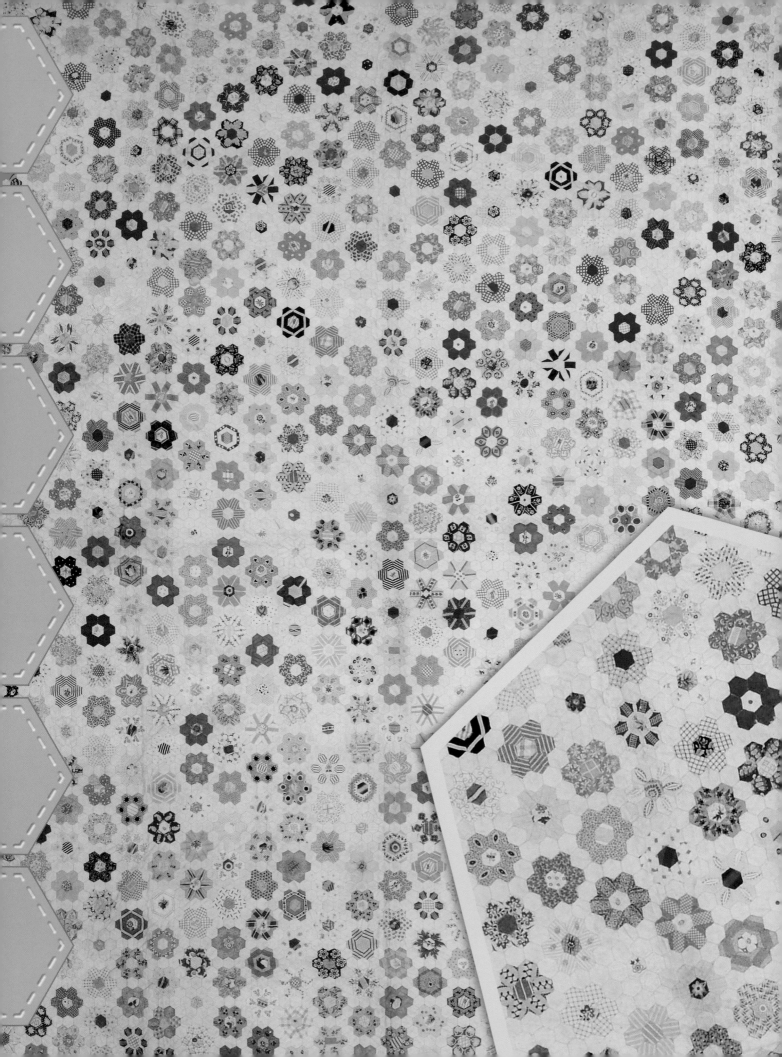

contents

Introduction 6

Appreciating Pieces from the Past 8

Chapter One: Hexies as Sashing 22

Chapter Two: Hexies as Blocks 32

Chapter Three: Square in a Square 40

Chapter Four: Playing With Edges 46

Chapter Five: Fusible is Your Friend 50

Chapter Six: Offset Settings 54

Chapter Seven: A Simple Border 60

Chapter Eight: Mixing it Up 74

Chapter Nine: Pillow Talk 84

Chapter Ten: Working with Vintage Hexie Fabrics 90

Chapter Eleven: Labels and Documentation 96

Chapter Twelve: Variations in Quilting 100

Epilogue 102

Professional Quilters 108

Index 109

About the Author 111

Mosaic, circa 1820, 55 x 78".
This quilt is in the collection
of Sue Reich

introduction

For as long as women have been quilting, there have been projects left undone. Some quilts were never finished because of time constraints, others were not of the quality of workmanship desired, and still others were simply victims of a woman's prerogative to change her mind. I have always been drawn to these unfinished projects and have collected blocks, tops, and fragments for many years. Hexagons are my favorite pattern and I love the challenge of incorporating this versatile shape into my contemporary quilting. The idea of recycling these fabrics simply makes my heart sing!

Some tops were sturdy enough to finish into quilts while others had suffered years of abuse and neglect. Many tops were never finished, and still others languished as orphan blocks. My mission was to repurpose these fragments of yesterday into something that can be used and enjoyed for generations to come. I love the opportunity to combine blocks, attempt an innovative setting, or create a small quilt that showcases a limited number of blocks. I celebrate the quilters who came before me and pay homage to the quilting traditions they passed on to us.

Thank you to my editors, Nancy Schiffer and Cheryl Weber, and the staff at Schiffer Publishing, Ltd., for their encouragement and support. Thank you to Barb Garrett and Sue Reich for their generous assistance with photography. Thank you to my sister, Karen Mitchell, for reading the manuscript in progress and helping to organize my thoughts. Thank you to the many friends who stepped in to help as I scrambled to completed the more than 50 quilts created for this book. And last, but not least, thank you to my family and to the women in my life who serve as my army of cheerleaders. Life would not be the same without you!

Mary Kerr
www.MaryWKerr.com

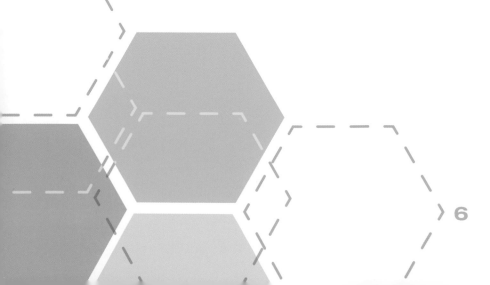

6

Mosaic top, circa 1890,
62 x 96". This quilt is in the
collection of Mary Kerr.

appreciating pieces from the past

The simple hexagon has been a staple in our quilting traditions for more than 300 years. Early patterns employed this versatile shape in quilts we know as Mosiac or Honeycomb. In the twentieth century, this hexagon piecing became known as Grandmother's Flower Garden.

The basic shape has not changed over time but the fabric choices, piecing methods, and overall designs reflect the resources that were available to each maker in her time. Researchers have written volumes on the wonderful antique art pieces created through the years. Museums treasure these intricate designs and their exhibits continue to inspire quilters today.

My love of the hexie design style began with an appreciation of these historical textiles. I am honored to share a few of my favorite pieces.

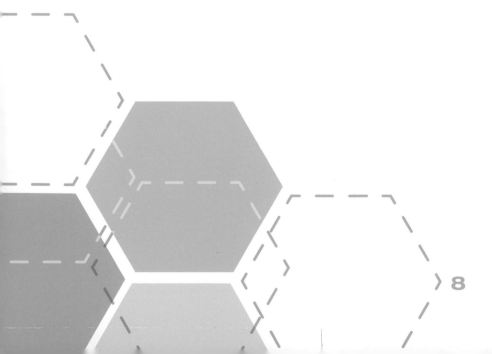

Paper pieced hexagon block with papers intact, circa 1840.

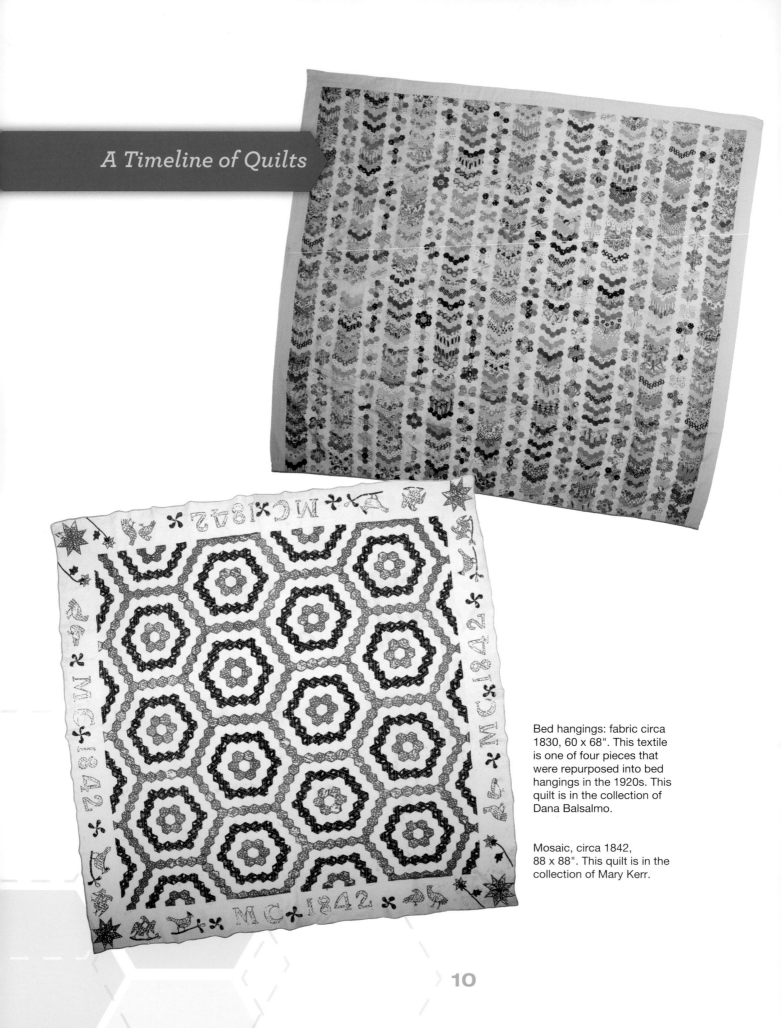

Bed hangings: fabric circa 1830, 60 x 68". This textile is one of four pieces that were repurposed into bed hangings in the 1920s. This quilt is in the collection of Dana Balsalmo.

Mosaic, circa 1842, 88 x 88". This quilt is in the collection of Mary Kerr.

Mosaic Diamonds, circa 1840, 74 x 80". This quilt is in the collection of Dana Balsalmo.

Mosaic Star, circa 1850, 88 x 99". This quilt is in the collection of Mary Kerr.

Mosaic Diamonds, circa 1860,
82 x 84". This quilt is in the collection
of Dana Balsalmo.

Mosaic scrappy quilt,
circa 1870, 76 x 78". This
quilt is in the collection of
Mary Kerr.

Mosaic Diamonds,
circa 1860,
62 x 64". This quilt is in
the collection of Dana
Balsalmo.

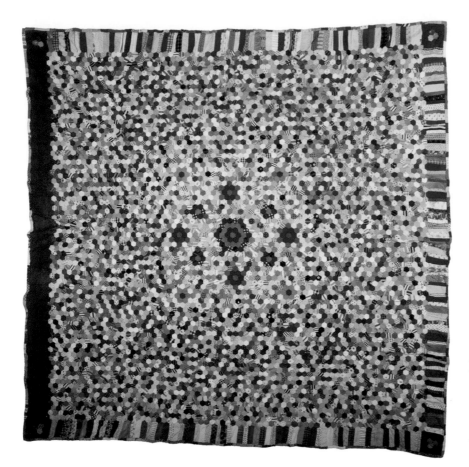

Mosaic, circa 1880,
88 x 89". This quilt is in
the collection of Mary Kerr.

Mosaic Star, circa 1890,
71 x 76". This quilt is in the
collection of Bunnie Jordan.

14

Mosaic with flour sack backing, circa 1890, 60 x 82". This quilt is in the collection of Mary Kerr.

Grandmother's Flower Garden, circa 1925, 84 x 90". This quilt is in the collection of Mary Kerr.

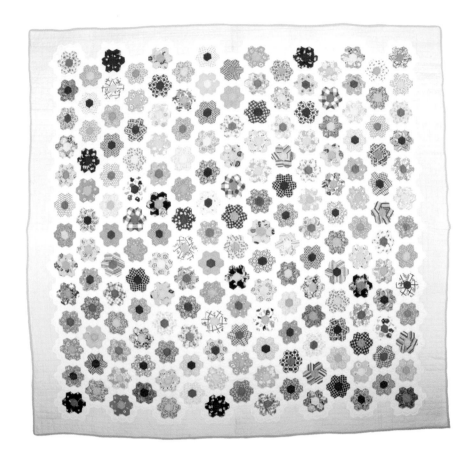

Grandmother's Flower Garden, made by Abalona Klein of St Marys, Kansas, in 1924, 80 x 80". This quilt is in the collection of Mary Kerr.

Grandmother's Flower Garden, circa 1930, 70 x 90". This quilt is in the collection of Patricia Andrews.

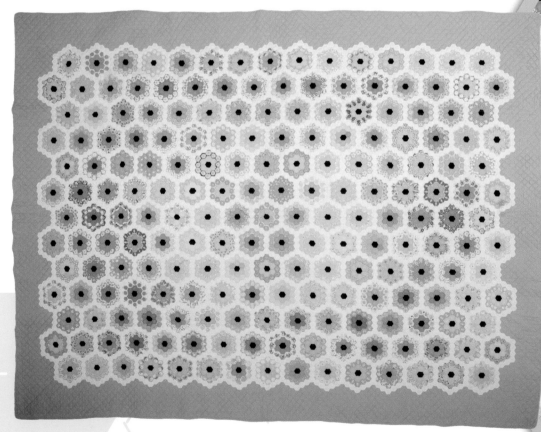

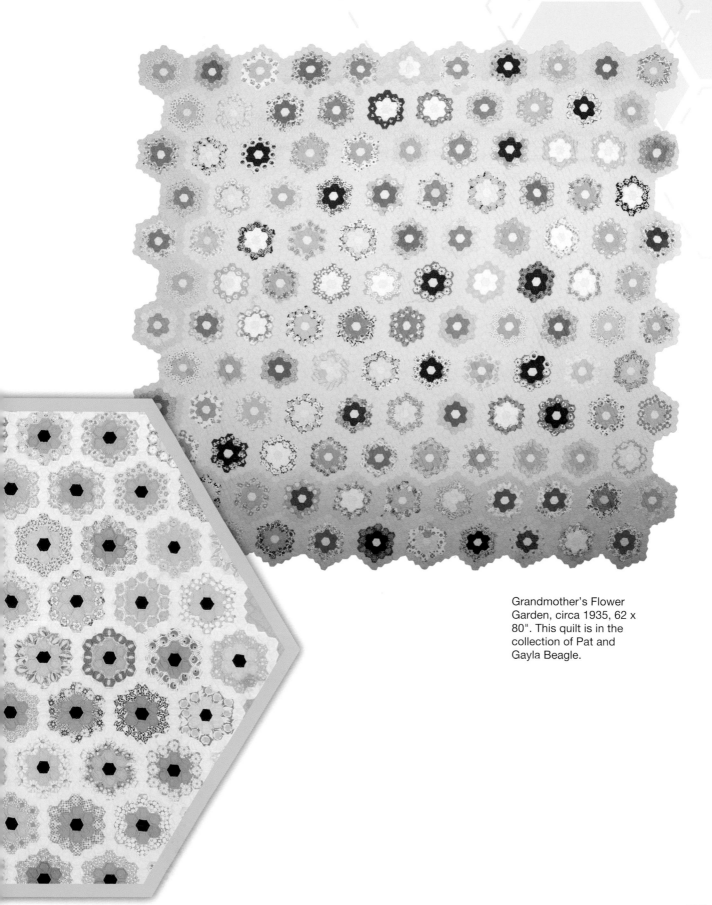

Grandmother's Flower Garden, circa 1935, 62 x 80". This quilt is in the collection of Pat and Gayla Beagle.

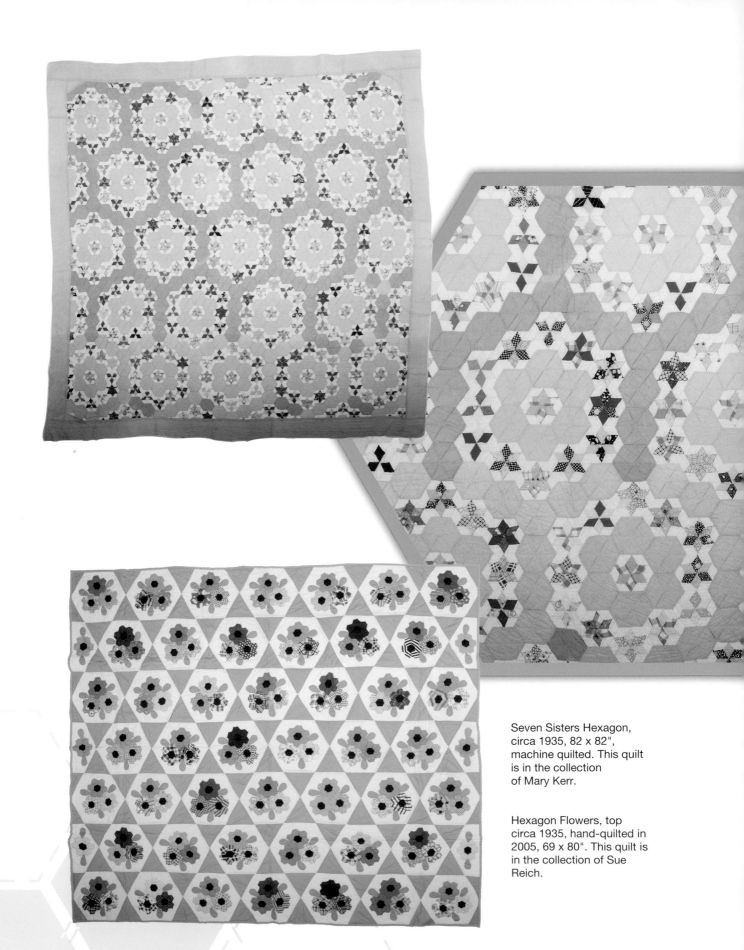

Seven Sisters Hexagon, circa 1935, 82 x 82", machine quilted. This quilt is in the collection of Mary Kerr.

Hexagon Flowers, top circa 1935, hand-quilted in 2005, 69 x 80". This quilt is in the collection of Sue Reich.

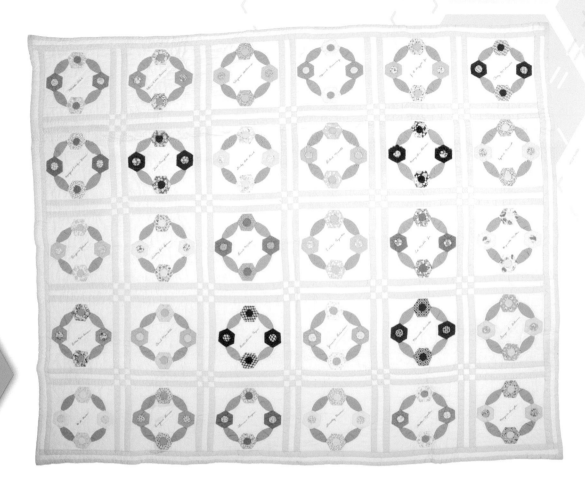

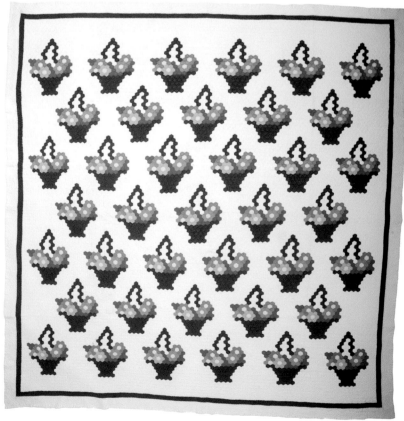

Hexagon Wreath,
circa 1935, 66 x 81".
This quilt is in the
collection of
Sue Reich.

Hexagon Basket,
made by Erma Fortna
in 1938, 88 x 92".
This quilt is in the
collection of
Dorothy Fortna.

Hexagon variation, circa 1940, 74 x 85". This quilt is in the collection of Mary Kerr.

Hexagon Basket, circa 1940, 74 x 87". This quilt is in the collection of Sue Reich.

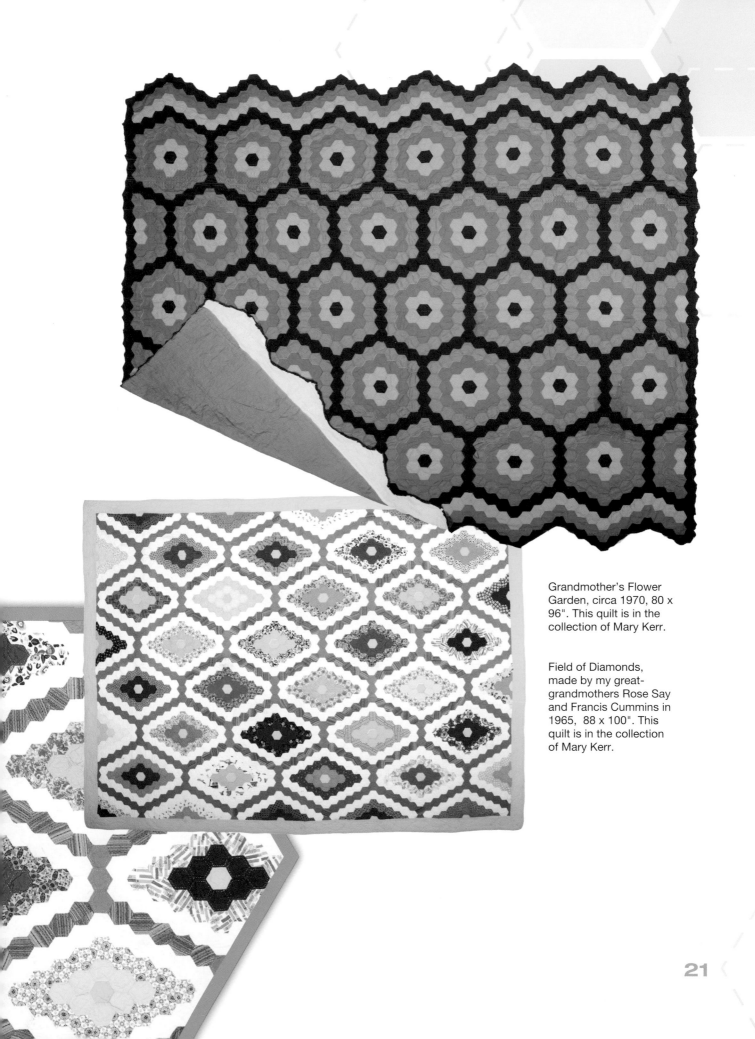

Grandmother's Flower Garden, circa 1970, 80 x 96". This quilt is in the collection of Mary Kerr.

Field of Diamonds, made by my great-grandmothers Rose Say and Francis Cummins in 1965, 88 x 100". This quilt is in the collection of Mary Kerr.

One of the simplest ways to incorporate vintage hexie fabrics into your quilt is to use them as sashing between other blocks. The narrow strips allow you to manipulate color placement and patterns while working around any damaged area in the original textile.

Care needs to be taken so that the hexie textiles lay flat and are not stretched. The use of cornerstones allows shorter pieces to be included and provides a great place for a small pop of color.

hexies as
SASHING

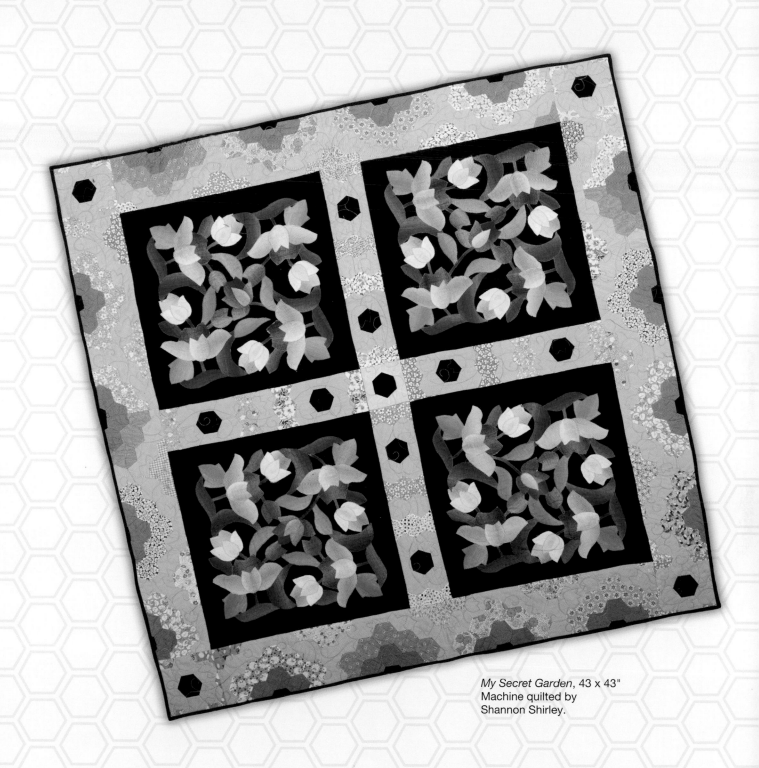

My Secret Garden, 43 x 43"
Machine quilted by
Shannon Shirley.

The blocks can be new, as seen in *My Secret Garden*. These applique blocks were purchased from an unknown maker on eBay®. They are not high-quality, yet their bright colors pair wonderfully with the back setting fabric and fussy cut borders.

Other blocks are from sets of orphan blocks, as seen in *Nine Little Ducks*. Originally there were eleven vintage duck blocks that look oddly like a cross between a duck and a chicken. They were badly stained and needed to be pretreated before being incorporated into this cheerful quilt. The placement of the orange hexie blocks creates a unique secondary design. I often use leftover quilt fragments on the back fabric, if possible. Here you can imagine what the original top looked like.

HINT

Restoration and Retro Clean are both excellent products to brighten up yellowed blocks and remove stains.

Nine Little Ducks, 37 x 37"
Machine quilted by Ginny Rippe.

Love Everlasting, 54 x 54".
Machine quilted by Jane Miller.

    The embroidered blocks used in *Love Everlasting* were originally part of a damaged quilt top. Twelve of the fifteen blocks were salvaged; nine are shown in *Love Everlasting*, and a single block is featured in *Choices*. The maker of this hexagon fragment wrote her initials in pencil in multiple places on this top. The letters L.E. inspired the name *Love Everlasting*, and quilter Jane Miller carefully embroidered each set of initials and added them to the cornerstones. Only after this quilt was completed did we notice her name, Lenore, penciled on the quilt back.

Choices, 20 x 20".
Machine quilted by
Mary Kerr.

Hexie top fragment
used in *Choices*.

Four floral appliqué blocks were used to create *A Summer Breeze*. These were from a set of seven blocks rescued from an antique dealer in the Midwest. Four blocks are shown here, and the remaining three are featured in *My Lovely Purple Garden* (seen on page 44).

A Summer Breeze, 45 x 45".
Machine quilted by Kelly Kline.

With Love from Arline,
36 x 32 ½". Machine
quilted by Vicki
Maloney.

I created *With Love from Arline* from parts of two dresser scarves and fragments of a hexie top. The thin embroidered linens were backed with interfacing for additional stability. My husband's aunt, Arline Hennighan, embroidered them in the 1950s; they were two of the linens that she gifted me before her death in 2011.

My grandmother, Opal Wilson (1912-2007), was known for her extensive needle skills and love of every craft technique ever invented. She painted this pair of pillowcases using the Tri-Chem paints that were the rage in the 1950s. The cases were well-loved and worn, yet the painted edges could be salvaged and incorporated into this memory piece, *Roses for Opal*. Vintage 1920s pink fabric is paired with bright hexagon fabrics from the 1930s. Mixing eras just creates a more interesting piece and a much better story!

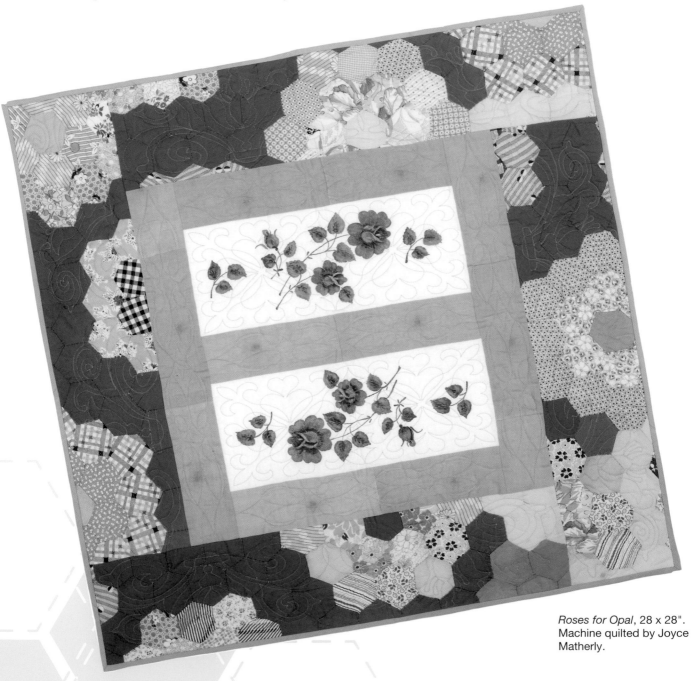

Roses for Opal, 28 x 28".
Machine quilted by Joyce
Matherly.

Painted pillowcases used in
Roses for Opal.

Sometimes vintage hexie textiles can simply be cut into squares and incorporated into the quilt in place of a solid fabric piece. Any pattern with a geometric shape can be adapted to showcase pieced hexies.

hexies as
BLOCKS

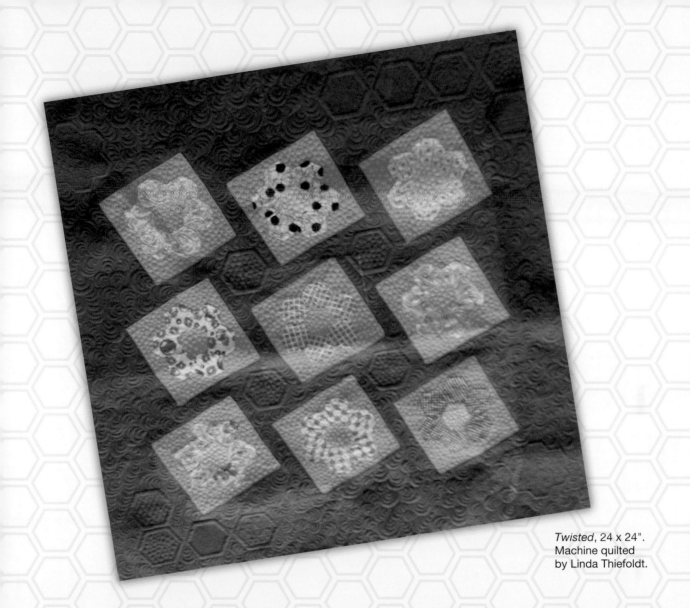

Twisted, 24 x 24".
Machine quilted
by Linda Thiefoldt.

Twisted is a wonderful play on the skewed squares technique. Six-inch squares were cut from a hexie top fragment and sashed with elongated triangles to create a twisted square. A simple frame that matched the setting fabric results in a design that seems to dance across the quilt.

I created *Lancaster* using Ann Holt's Lancaster Diamond template produced by Quilter's Rule. This template was designed after Ann researched an antique quilt found in Lancaster, Pennsylvania, that incorporated leftover blocks in a 65-degree diamond. I paired a fragment of a 1940s Grandmother's Flower Garden top with vintage lavender and purple solids.

Lancaster, 34 ½ x 42".
Machine quilted by
M&M Quilting.

Baby Blue, 33" x 33".
Hand quilted by Didi Salvatierra.

Baby Blue was designed to showcase a set of eight appliqué blocks from the 1920s. The original pattern called for 64 blocks, but the maker finished only a portion. The Daisy blocks were found with the pattern from 1924, along with some of the fabric needed to complete the project. Fragments of a tied hexie quilt were cut into the same-size squares and set on point with sashing and small cornerstones. Small pieces of the top were pieced together to create the hexie border surrounding the mix of blocks.

Four 1940s redwork embroidery blocks, a vintage dress bodice, and fragments of an 1890s mosaic top are combined to create *Asian Elegance*. The embroidered blocks were set on point with large squares of this partial top. The side setting triangles started their life as part of a dress bodice. Debbie Kauffman's quilting elevates this striking piece to a place of elegance.

Asian Elegance, 53 ½ x 53 ½".
Machine-quilted by
Debbie Kauffman.

36

My Heart Soars, 25 x 25".
Hand quilted by Doris Bloomer.

My grandmother Kathryne Say (1912-2003) was a lifetime quilter and an accomplished needlewoman. She loved many things including her grandchildren, a mean card game, her garden, and the many birds that came to visit her feeders. She gifted me with four panels of Penny Square bird blocks that she embroidered in late 1930s. The colors she used varied depending on the available thread, and the panels were never finished. I created *My Heart Soars* by pairing the four bluebird blocks with a red, white, and blue unfinished hexie fragment from the 1940s. The birds, the sentiment, and Doris Bloomer's beautiful hand quilting make my heart take flight.

On a Roll combines my love of vintage hexies with some of the modern techniques in today's amazing quilt world. I paired a 1930s hexie quilt top fragment with a Moda Jelly Roll. These rolls of 2½-inch precut strips are available in a myriad of patterns and colors. I improvisationally pieced the blocks using modern quilt movement techniques, with a hexie quilt scrap as the offset center square. One jelly roll + hexie scrap = magic.

On a Roll, 51 x 51". Machine quilted
by Marla Margelewski.

Hexie fragment used in
On a Roll.

Square-in-a-square block placement and side setting triangles allow a single block to shine on a bigger stage. The normal practice here is to ensure that the outside edges are on the straight grain of the fabric. This is difficult when working with hexie textiles, so additional tricks may be needed.

square in a
SQUARE

Hearts All Around, 27 x 27".
Hand quilted by Doris Bloomer.

I typically cut my setting triangles larger than necessary to allow for distortion, and trim later. The hexie rule for half-square triangles is to add 1 ½ inches to the finished side measurement on the triangle leg (the two sides that end in a 90-degree corner). Cut the two squares in half along the diagonal to create four triangles. Center one of the longer triangle edges to one side of your square with right sides together and the hexie piecing on the bottom, using your square's straight edge as a guideline for sewing. I start with a partial seam, press towards the middle and move in a clockwise direction, adding each piece and pressing. My last row of stitching completes the partial seam. I then trim to a perfect square and add additional borders if desired.

Hearts All Around is a single vintage block bordered by hexie fragments and hand quilted. The precise piecing of this 1900 mosaic fragment beautifully balances the folk art charm of the crooked appliqué block.

May Dance features a delightful embroidered scene. I found the tiny embroidery scrap on the corner of a tattered tablecloth, and this was the only orientation that would work without extensive piecing. I paired it with cut-out triangles from a hexie top fragment and finished it with a simple yellow border. For the facing, I chose an 11 by 11-inch piece that allows the hexie scraps to peek through on the back. This is a great way to use small pieces for big impact.

May Dance, 11 x 11".
Machine quilted by Jane Hamilton.

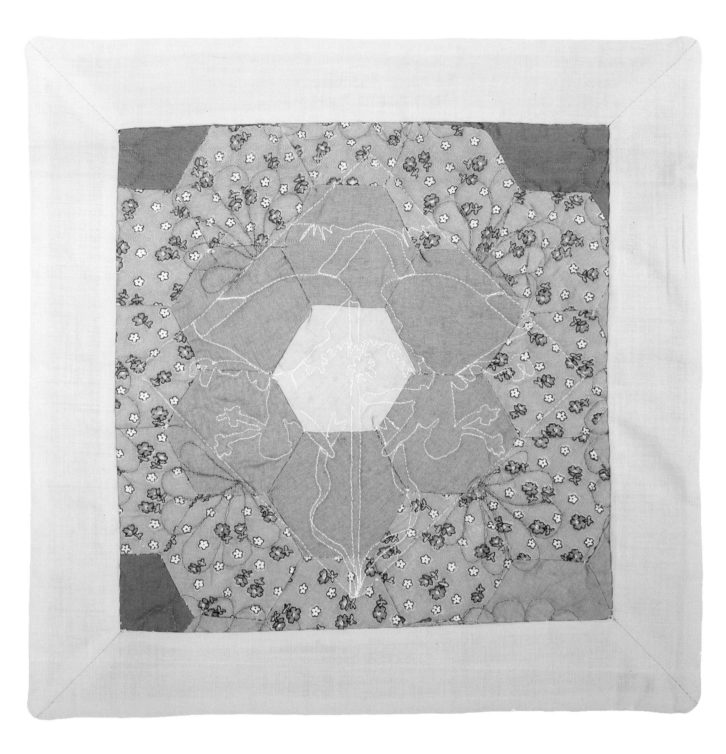

Back of *May Dance.*

I expanded on this technique in *My Lovely Purple Garden*, where the center appliqué block is embellished with a green flange and bordered with pieces of companion blocks. The extra appliqué blocks were fussy cut and pieced to form the outer border. Leftover units appear on the back.

HINT

A flange is a great way to add a pop of color and separate the units. One-inch strips are folded in half and inserted into the seam. Sew the raw edges of the folded fabric along the seam line and then piece as normal. To hide the stitches, move the needle on your machine one step to the left.

My Lovely Purple Garden, 29 x 29". Machine quilted by Debbie Kauffman.

Butterscotch, 46 x 46".
Machine quilted by
Barbara Dann.

Butterscotch showcases a single appliqué block. The vintage block has been bordered with two layers of square-in-a-square treatments with a soft yellow solid to separate and highlight the units. The backing fabric is a bright yellow feedsack.

4

Many of the surviving embroidered linen pieces are embellished with a decorative edging. This may be crocheted, tatted, braided, or embellished with trim. Working with several of these pieces, I was challenged to find a way to incorporate the edges without using the entire textile.

playing with
EDGES

At the Barre, 22 x 20".
Machine quilted by
Shannon Shirley.

At the Barre uses the entire width of a dresser scarf depicting a graceful ballerina at its edge. The trimmed end of the textile was simply inserted into the outer quilt border and the decorative edge was tacked down over the existing base—a black rectangle bordered with fragments of a Grandmother's Flower Garden top. Shannon Shirley expertly added a dancer's stage and curtains in the quilting stitches.

Both *Sleepytime* and *Edisto* feature linen fragments pieced into a top so that the decorative edging would be shown. The center part of the top was first pieced in three vertical segments. An extra layer of coordinating fabric was pinned to the vintage linen just under the decorative edge to complete the length of the outside borders. The sides of this extra fabric were caught in the seams and the top open edge hidden by the vintage linen. Finally, the top and bottom borders were added and the decorative edge was tacked down by hand or machine.

Sleepytime, 18 ½ x 19". Hand quilted by Doris Bloomer.

Edisto, 15 x 16". Machine quilted by Jane Hamilton.

My Basket Overflows, 26 x 28".
Unfinished top.

  My Basket Overflows is a piece in progress featuring the decorative edge of a vintage Grandmother's Flower Garden top. Evidently, this top had been appliquéd to a border fabric at one time and the beautiful edges were still perfectly turned under. The center was shattered, so I carefully pieced the four corners of the top and used them to showcase this embroidered basket of flowers.

5

If you take your pieced hexagons apart, fusible interfacing and a good seam ripper are your best friends. Fusing the hexie units allows you to place them without piecing and add a pop of color or a new and exciting shape.

fusible is your
FRIEND

Watermelon Wonder, 31 x 23".
Machine quilted by Leslie Harris.

When dissecting the hexagon units, the goal is to save as much material as possible so the outer edges are not misshapen. For both hand and machine stitched seams, gently remove the stitches from the underside of the fabric by snipping every other thread and carefully separating the seams. Do not try to rip the seam or pull a long thread, which will distort the fabric.

These hexagon units can be easily used if you iron them to fusible interfacing. Leave the edges raw, trimming them after you add the interfacing. This adds stability to thin fabrics and helps prevent further distortion. After the piece is attached to your quilt, cover the edges with decorative stitches or secure with the quilting stitches.

My Grandma Kay painted this pair of kitchen towels in the 1950s and then tucked them away unused. *Watermelon Wonder* celebrates my grandmother's love of this summer fruit and the joy of those long, busy days. I paired the painted pieces with hand-dyed cotton and embellished the border with fused hexie units from the 1940s.

Galaxy, 32 x 32". Machine
quilted by Stephanie Adams.

Galaxy was created when large diamond shapes were arranged in a star on a
black background. These diamonds were liberated from a top in which the pink
setting path fabric had run and discolored many of the fabrics around it. Removing
the diamonds from the top allowed me the freedom to place them in a variety of
designs and settings.

Twist and Shout was pieced in the same manner as *Twisted* (page 33). Squares of a patriotic Grandmother's Flower Garden fragment were sashed with long triangles to create a twisted square. Additional flower units were fused around the wide border and finished with a machine buttonhole stitch. Vicki Maloney's longarm quilting makes these squares seem to dance.

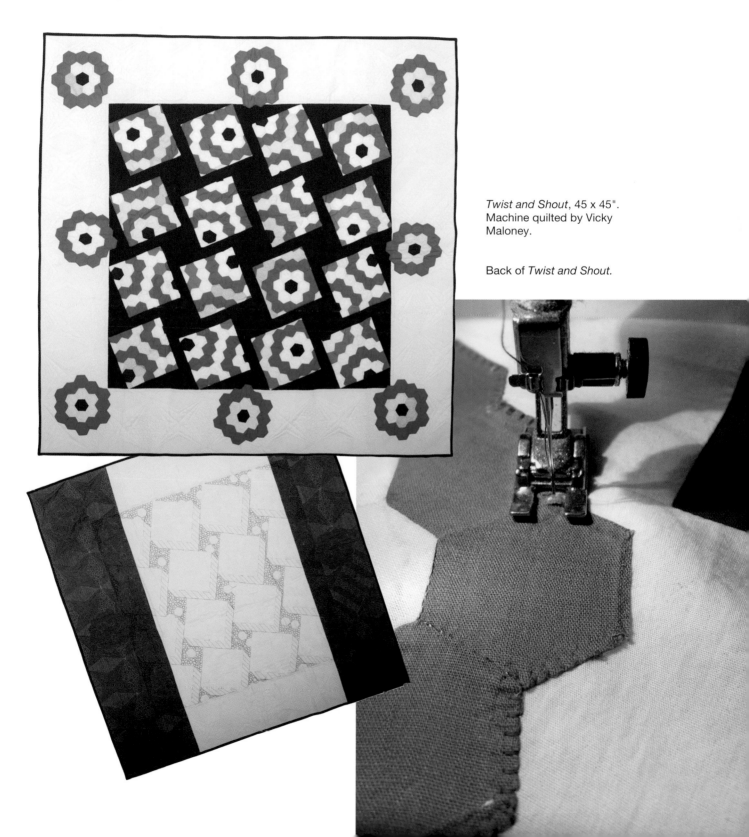

Twist and Shout, 45 x 45".
Machine quilted by Vicky Maloney.

Back of *Twist and Shout*.

6

At times, an asymmetrical setting is the perfect way to showcase a vintage linen or single block. These settings provide the opportunity to use a larger hexie top fragment.

offset
SETTINGS

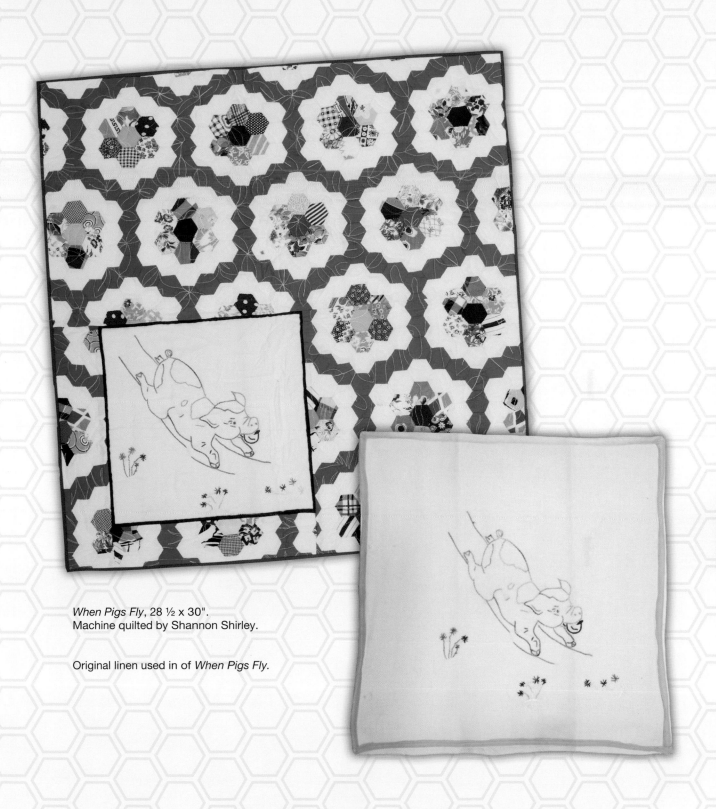

When Pigs Fly, 28 ½ x 30".
Machine quilted by Shannon Shirley.

Original linen used in of *When Pigs Fly*.

These next two quilts use hexie fabric from the same partial Grandmother's Flower Garden top. The size of this long, thin piece determined the width of *When Pigs Fly*. *An Apple a Day* was pieced from the leftover fabrics. My quilters added their own special touches to these quilts. Shannon Shirley quilted a farm scene behind the embroidered pig, a quilted tree, and apple hexies throughout. Sarah Entsminger added button embellishments to the sweet dog embroidery and chose a vintage apple backing fabric.

An Apple a Day, 17 x 16".
Machine quilted by
Sarah Entsminger.

Hexie top used in When Pigs
Fly and *An Apple a Day*.

Bali Fish combines a contemporary batik fish panel with fragments of a mosaic top from the last quarter of the nineteenth century. This partial top was gifted to me in segments, as there was extensive damage in several areas of the textile. After the piece was quilted, I added eyelash trim for a pop of color and to soften the transition between the panel and mosaic top.

Bali Fish, 25 x 26". Machine quilted by Shannon Shirley.

Picnic showcases a single large 1940's hexagon fused asymmetrically onto a vintage tablecloth. I love the modern feel of the large hexie units when paired with Sue Papalia's quilting.

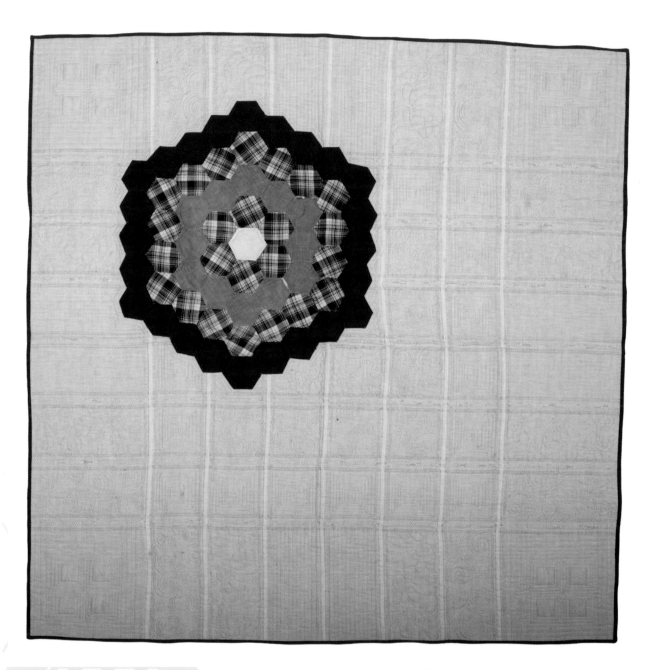

Picnic, 51 x 51". Machine quilted by Sue Papalia.

Detail of *Picnic*.

HINT

Explore ways of incorporating other vintage textiles into your recycled hexie pieces. A vintage tablecloth is a great backdrop and vintage feedsacks are often the perfect color you are looking for. Scraps of clothing, old aprons, ties, and bed linens have all found their way into my quilts.

7

A simple border is often the most effective way to feature a vintage linen or a single treasured block. There is no set formula, and I find that auditioning pieces before cutting works well for me. The border size will vary, depending on your vision and the amount of fabric on hand. Many of my piecing decisions are determined by the amount and quality of the available materials.

a simple
BORDER

Lovebirds, 32 x 32".
Machine quilted
by Kelly Cline.

When using recycled hexie fabrics, I often work around damaged areas and stains. I am constantly moving pieces to find the right color placement. A cleared table or my ironing board allows me to position before cutting in order to find the fabric and pattern that works best. For long seams, I pin the center to the border fabric and stitch using the center fabric edge as my guide. After the seam is in place, I go back and trim the hexie fabric to ¼-inch seam allowance and press towards the center. This prevents distortion and stretching of edges.

Lovebirds pairs a red embroidered block from the 1940s with a fragment of an 1890 mosaic top. This simplest of presentations allows the beautiful stitching, bold colors, and period fabrics to shine.

Summer Morning follows this same minimalist style with a vintage table runner and fragments of a larger-scale Field of Diamonds pattern from the 1940's. This top had never been completed and its sturdy fabrics allowed me to use an extra-wide border. The inaccuracies in piecing caused the fabric to buckle slightly, so it demanded dense machine quilting to achieve a flat finish.

Summer Morning, 35 x 51½".
Machine quilted by Sue Papalia.

Eat Your Fruit, 26 x 51".
Machine quilted by Joyce Matherly.

Eat Your Fruit features another vintage table runner produced by Vogart Patterns in the 1940s. It is framed by a gold border and a randomly pieced 1930s hexagon top. The hexie fragments were very thin and I had to carefully avoid the damaged areas. I added a second fabric layer under the top for quilting stability.

Fragments of a tied baby quilt were paired with a favorite Vogart pillowtop to create *Love My Banjo Boy* in honor of my banjo-playing husband. I pieced the Vogart label into the quilt back and made a label with the remaining hexie fragments.

Love My Banjo Boy,
25 x 20 ½". Machine quilted
by Shannon Shirley.

Hexie top and Vogart
top used for *Love My
Banjo Boy.*

Georgia incorporates a vintage cutwork doily into a simple bordered frame. To create this quilted frame, I first had to determine the finished size for my focus doily. I cut the center background square and added the 1900s hexie fragments as borders. This base was quilted and bound, and then the vintage linen was attached by machine. I used matching thread and an open toe foot to hide the stitches when sewing down the decorative linen.

Georgia, 32 x 32 ".
Hand quilted by Doris Bloomer.

Let's Dance! 14 x 12 ½ ".
Hand quilted by Dawn Jolin.

Let's Dance is a small piece bordered with fabric from two single hexagon blocks that my grandmother pieced in the 1940s. I cut the long borders through the center of the blocks and cut the top and bottom border pieces from the remaining fabric. A black flange and an outer back border add an elegant touch. The backing is vintage family fabric.

Mary, Mary is another tiny piece whose size was determined by the small quantity of fabric I had available. As you can see in this picture, the top was tattered and worn. I simply quilted the fragile fabrics and added a fun music print to the back. A single hexie flower was fused in one corner and stitched down by machine.

Mary, Mary, 8 x 8 ½".
Machine quilted by Mary Kerr.

Back of *Mary, Mary*.

Hexie top and
embroidered linen
used for *Mary, Mary*.

HINT

Be adventurous with your backing fabrics. I love the surprise of a novelty print or vintage textile, top, or fragment. Backings are a great way to use older fabrics in your stash.

These next two quilts are both small pieces with big visual impacts. One can't help but smile at the sight of this miniature elephant with his guitar or the regal flamingo. In *Let's Boogie,* the hexie fabric is encased in an outer solid border, while *Flamingo* had an inner border followed by the larger hexie fragments. The recipe for success is always changing.

Let's Boogie, 11 x 14". Machine quilted by Shannon Shirley.

Flamingo, 13 x 17". Machine quilted by Jane Hamilton.

Dinnertime, 17 x 19". Hand quilted by Doris Bloomer.

Dinnertime features a vintage embroidery surrounded by a series of solid borders, hexie fragments, and flanges. Sometimes we need to mix it up and try different things. When I sent this piece to Doris Bloomer to be hand quilted, it had a solid black border that was later removed to lighten up the composition. The extra border needed to go! Lesson learned—it is okay to change your mind.

Wine with Friends, 23 x 23".
Machine quilted by Shannon Shirley.

Wine With Friends started as an unfinished 1930s Vogart pillow top. The embroidery was never completed, yet I chose to leave it unfinished and pair it with hexie fragments from the same era. I pieced the outer border to create enough yardage from the remnants of this Grandmother's Flower Garden top. Shannon Shirley's background quilting created a cozy room setting and the word "Cheers." Few things are sweeter than time spent with special friends.

Sometimes a top doesn't turn out the way you envisioned and can benefit from a fresh pair of eyes. This daffodil block was bordered with fragments of a tattered worn hexie top. I loved the green, but there was not enough other color that could be salvaged to make the border anywhere near symmetrical. Debbie Dempsey took this top to quilt and quietly asked if she could add to it. *Daffodil's Delight* was born when Debbie's art quilter eye worked magic with the addition of vintage lace, sheer leaves, beads, threadwork, and pigma pen.

Daffodil's Delight, 30 ½ x 30 ½". Machine quilted and embellished by Debbie Dempsey.

73

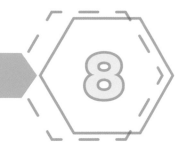

8

I enjoy the challenge of working with textiles that combine different colors, patterns, and designs. Bringing pieces together that started their lives in different homes makes me smile. The process is a happy collaboration with lots of trial and error. I start by gathering pieces that I think might look good together—linens, blocks, top fragments, etc. I often carry a block with me to fabric shops or antique stores in search of that perfect match.

mixing it
UP

Apron Strings, 30 x 31".
Machine quilted by Marty Vint.

HINT

Use a digital camera to take pictures as you work. This gives you a point of reference to return to and lets you rearrange pieces without fear of forgetting previous arrangements.

The quilts in this chapter are a combination of the techniques shared elsewhere in this book. I generally work from the center and add borders until the quilt tells me to stop. I do not work from a preset plan and I often change design direction as I work. I encourage my students to gather pieces they enjoy and then give themselves permission to play.

Apron Strings combines a vintage embroidery piece with two different top fragments. The inner section is a 1940s Grandmother's Flower Garden fragment that was pieced with heavy cotton. To preserve the pattern, I appliquéd the sashed embroidery directly onto the hexie fragment. I gave it a pink border and finished it with a wide border of a remnant Hearts and Gizzards top from the 1920s.

My husband's aunt, Arline Hennighan, loved us dearly. She had no children of her own, yet spent many years spoiling her nieces, nephews, and godchildren. She traveled with us frequently in the last years of her life, and the Arline stories are legendary. After she gave me a pair of dresser scarves years ago, I struggled to create a fitting memorial for this special lady. *Arline's Basket* features two different hexie top fragments. One is from the 1930s and the other was part of an unfinished top from the 1940s. *A Basketful of Hugs* is simply bordered with one of these top fragments and a vintage cotton print. Both feature Arline's labels and her signature hugs.

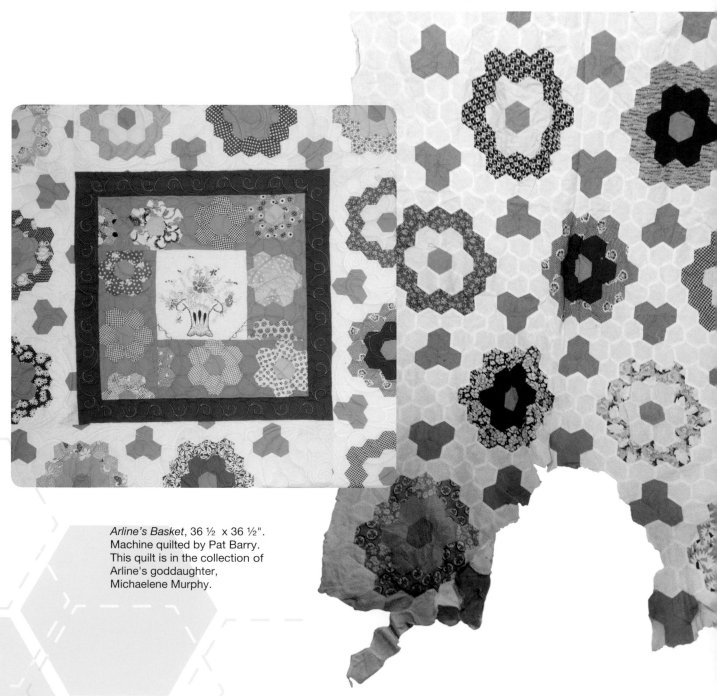

Arline's Basket, 36 ½ x 36 ½".
Machine quilted by Pat Barry.
This quilt is in the collection of
Arline's goddaughter,
Michaelene Murphy.

A Basketful of Hugs, 18 x 18". Machine quilted by Joyce Matherly. This quilt is in the collection of Arline's great-neice, Katherine Kerr McPherson.

When a friend was downsizing, these poorly made flying geese blocks from about 1900 came to live at my house. I left the center block intact and took apart the others to create the pieced border of this quilt. I embraced the wonky blocks, added my hexies, and did not try to remove the gathers or reinstate the lost points. "Wonky" was my friend and I was determined to make these work. *Flying Home to Teddy* celebrates the make-do attitude of quilters and our willingness to work with what is in front of us.

Flying Home to Teddy, 37 x 37"
Machine quilted by Sue Papalia.

Stars for Grandma Kay, 68 x 68".
Hand quilted by Didi Salvatierra.

I created *Stars for Grandma Kay* to showcase an appliqué piece on black that was part of my grandmother's collection. I challenged myself to use vintage solids and fragments of this damaged 1930s Grandmother's Flower Garden top. I loved the back centers and the elegant way they danced in the green paths. I used my square-in-a-square technique with multiple pieced borders of half-square triangles and pieced stars. The back is pieced with a larger fragment of the original top.

Orange You Glad You're Mine? was made to celebrate my daughter Katherine's 18th birthday in 2004. It was one of my first quilts to embrace recycled hexie designs. I paired orange blocks dating from 1840 to 1940 with a 1930s Flower Garden top, new red fabrics, and embroidered edges from a family linen. Fused hexagon blocks decorate the back in an exuberant splash of color.

Orange You Glad You're Mine? 75 x 75". Hand quilted by Didi Salvatierra.

HINT

Corner treatments are a great way to showcase the edge of a treasured linen. Insert the edge in a corner seam and pin it out of the way while quilting. Secure the decorative edges later with small buttons or hidden stitches.

Pastel Pretty, 55 x 55".
Machine quilted by Marty Vint.

This hexie top arrived in two pieces. Someone had cut a bed-size top straight down the middle. *Pastel Pretty* was born when I paired pieces of this top with some very uncircular circle blocks from the same 1930s era. This was one of the first vintage pieces that I had finished by machine, and the stunning contrast opened a whole new world of possibilities for me. I finished it with a piped edge using Susan Cleveland's Groovin' Piping Trimming® tool.

10

Some vintage hexagon fabrics are in pristine condition, but these are not the pieces I choose to work with in my recycling projects. I am drawn to fabrics that have been exposed to wear and tear, abuse and misuse. Ripped seams and frayed edges are common, while other pieces are stained or torn. Many have simply never been completed.

working with
vintage hexie
FABRICS

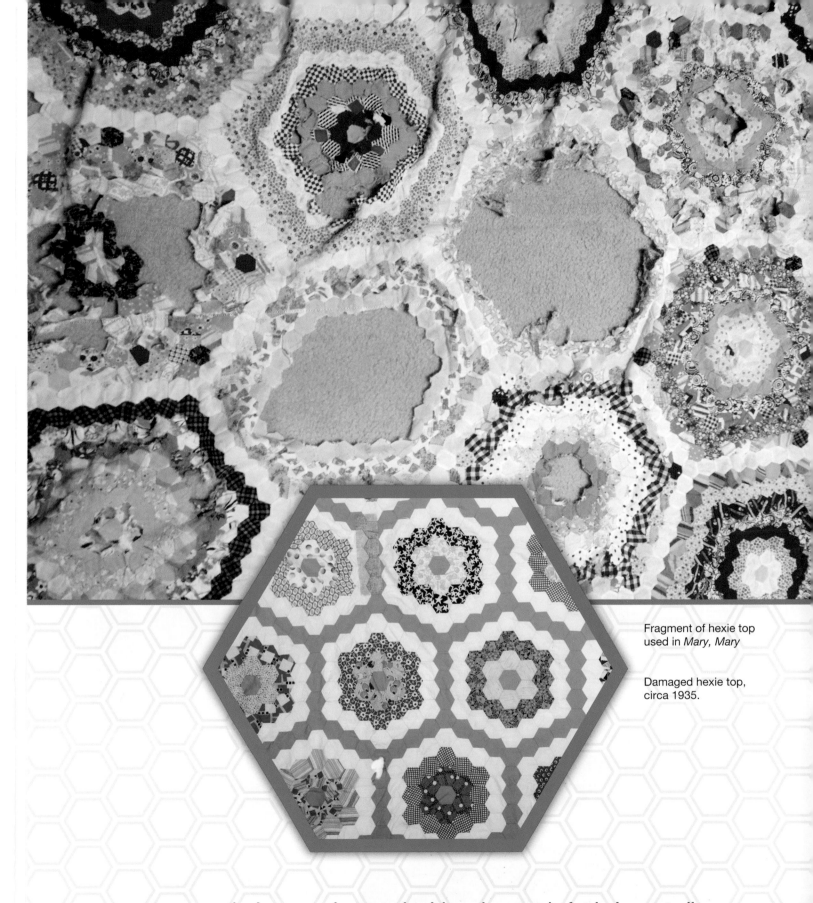

Fragment of hexie top used in *Mary, Mary*

Damaged hexie top, circa 1935.

Sometimes the damage can be repaired and the quilt top may be finished as originally intended. You can carefully clean the textile. Edges can be reinforced and separating seams can be resewn. Holes can be patched and missing fabric replaced.

11

As contemporary quilters, we have been told over and over that our quilts need to be labeled. At minimum, we are instructed to provide the maker's name, the quilter's name, and the year the quilt was made. There are a number of ways to create these labels, ranging from very basic to elaborately embellished story cards.

labels and
DOCUMEN-
TATION

When we work with vintage pieces, I feel we have an obligation to provide as much information as possible. I encourage my students to document everything they know about the textile and establish a connection to their intended recipient. Include circa dates for your fabrics and document what you used to create your quilt.

I frequently create labels using vintage blocks. I apply a fusible web to the back and write the information directly on the block with a fabric pen. I include the maker of the vintage linen, the date I created the piece, the quilter's name, and a note about what inspired me to make this quilt. The labels shown here are found on the backs of *Love My Banjo Boy*, *Stars for Grandma Kay*, *Pastel Pretty*, *Twist and Shout*, *Butterscotch*, *Galaxy*, and *My Secret Garden*.

Information can be written directly on a block before it is sewn to the quilt back. These extra blocks were used for *Nine Little Ducks*, *On a Roll*, and *Georgia*.

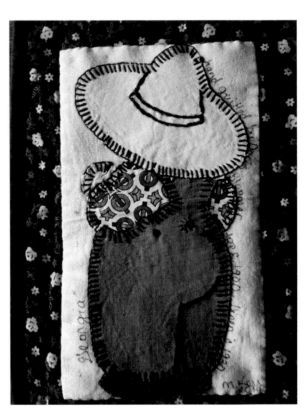

With Love from Arline

Arline Hennighan (1932-2011)

These embroidered linens were part
of a pair of dresser scarves created
by our Aunt Arline in the 1950's.
I paired the soaring birds with fragments
of a Grandmother's Flower Garden
top from the same era.

This quilt was created to celebrate her
youthful enthusiasm and her love of our family

Machine quilted by Vicki Maloney

Mary Kerr 2014

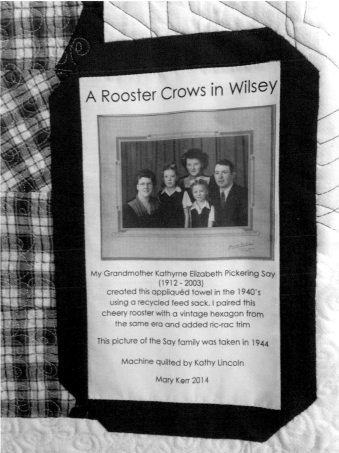

A Rooster Crows in Wilsey

My Grandmother Kathyrne Elizabeth Pickering Say
(1912 - 2003)
created this appliquéd towel in the 1940's
using a recycled feed sack. I paired this
cheery rooster with a vintage hexagon from
the same era and added ric-rac trim

This picture of the Say family was taken in 1944

Machine quilted by Kathy Lincoln

Mary Kerr 2014

Another wonderful option is to use photo transfer software to incorporate the maker's picture into your label. Scan a vintage photo into your computer, add supporting details, and print it onto photo transfer paper. I frame this label with strips of fabric and appliqué it to the back of the quilt. This technique allows us to preserve our cherished memories, passing them on to future generations. The labels shown here are on the backs of *With Love from Arline* and *A Rooster Crows in Wilsey*.

12

Quilting stitches are the glue that holds the textile together. These decorative stitches add definition, dimension, and another layer of design. How to finish a quilt is an age-old dilemma, and many of us struggle with these decisions. Fortunately, there are as many different ways to finish a quilt as there are quilters who work on them. Each individual brings unique talents and tastes to the worktable.

variations in
QUILTING

> 100

Detail of *Asian Elegance*,
quilted by Debbie Kauffman.

Detail of *Galaxy*,
quilted by Stephanie Adams.

I have finished quilts with almost every technique available. I love the look of hand quilting for some pieces, but others sing loudest with dense machine quilting. I enjoy the movement of wavy lines and I love the flow of an undulating feather.

All but a few of the quilts in this book were finished by others. I hand quilt when time allows, and I have experimented with various machine quilting techniques. However, I have long known that some members of my quilting community are far more talented stitchers than I am. What I love are the inspiration and design, and so now I ask others to quilt most of my pieces. I call this "quilting by check."

The quilters' names are listed prominently on my quilt labels, and they also should be credited in exhibition paperwork. I am thrilled to collaborate with these talented artists, and my work would not be the same without their talent.

epilogue

My recycled hexagon quilts have allowed me to discover one more way to pass on the gifts of our quilting heritage. Working with these special textiles, I am able to incorporate family heirlooms and perpetuate the memory of these special women who prepared our quilting paths. I am honored to walk in their footsteps.

Thank you for allowing me to share.

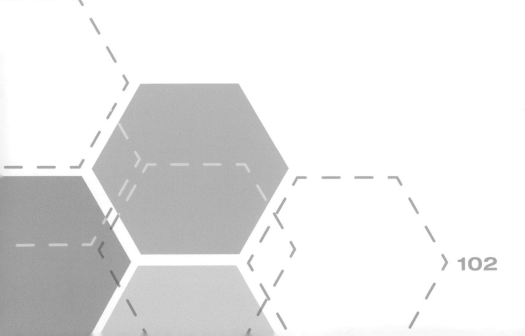

Vintage photograph, circa 1900.
This quilt is in the collection of Nancy Binder.

Vintage hexie top,
circa 1930.

Vintage hexie top,
circa 1940.

Vintage hexie top,
circa 1990.

My Lovely Purple Garden, 44
My Secret Garden, 23, 97
Nine Little Ducks, 24, 98
On a Roll, 38-39, 98
Orange You Glad You're Mine, 80
Painted linens, 30-31
Papalia, Sue, 58-59, 62, 78
Pastel Pretty, 81, 97
Patten, Sue, 1, 92
Picnic, 58-59
Pillows, 84-89
Professional Quilters, 108
Quilted Comfort, 85
Reich, Sue, 4-5, 18-20,
Rippe, Ginny, 24
Roses for Opal, 30-31
Salvatierra, Didi, 35, 79-80
Shirley, Shannon, 23, 47, 55, 57, 64-65, 70, 72
Sleepytime, 48
Stains, 93
Stars for Grandma Kay, 79, 97
Summer Morning, 62
Thiefoldt, Linda, 33
Tips to Remember, 95
Twist and Shout, 53, 97
Twisted, 33
Vint, Marty, 75, 81
Vintage quilt tops, 7, 92, 104–107, 110–111
Watermelon Wonder, 51
When Pigs Fly, 55-56
Wine with Friends, 72
With Love from Arline, 29, 99